LIFE AND LIMB

BY KEITH REDDIN

DRAMATISTS
PLAY SERVICE
INC.

LIFE AND LIMB

LIFE AND LIMB was presented by Playwrights Horizons, Andre Bishop, Artistic Director, on January 24, 1985. It was directed by Thomas Babe; scenery by John Arnone; costumes by David Woolard; lights by Steve Strawbridge. The stage manager was Melissa Davis.

The cast was as follows:

FRANKLIN CLAGG .... Robert Joy
EFFIE CLAGG .... Elizabeth Perkins
TOD CARTMELL .... Patrick Breen
DOINA FINDLEY .... Robin Bartlett
JERRY .... Thomas Toner
SAM .... Benjamin Hendrickson
ERIK .... Benjamin Hendrickson
GRANDFATHER .... Thomas Toner
CHRIS .... J. David Rozsa

LIFE AND LIMB was first presented as a staged reading at the 1983 National Playwrights Conference of the Eugene O'Neill Theatre Center. It was directed by John Pasquin. The world premiere production was at South Coast Repertory, January, 1984.

The play takes place during the years 1952–1956.

For Leslie

LIFE AND LIMB

ACT I

Scene One

A bench D. *Summer 1952. Franklin in uniform, Effie in print dress. Both face forward, sitting on bench. Early evening.*

EFFIE. Keep your eyes closed. (*Feeds him a spoonful of frozen custard.*) Guess what flavor.
FRANKLIN. Pistachio Fudge.
EFFIE. Be serious.
FRANKLIN. I'm serious, I'm very serious. (*He tastes a spoonful of custard.*) It was vanilla. You want another frozen custard?
EFFIE. No thanks.
FRANKLIN. How's about cotton candy?
EFFIE. You gonna make me sick, Franklin.
FRANKLIN. Go on.
EFFIE. I don't feel so good.
FRANKLIN. Gimme a kiss. (*They kiss.*) You don't use your tongue no more?
EFFIE. I told you I don't feel so good.
FRANKLIN. Always used to slip the tongue. I didn't grow up doing this.
EFFIE. Too many people around, Franklin. They looking at us.
FRANKLIN. I remember things like that.
EFFIE. It's the salt air too, makes me feel dizzy.
FRANKLIN. I got that surprise for you.
EFFIE. Was that where you was this afternoon?
FRANKLIN. You were with Doina. Going swimming, so I thought.
EFFIE. She thought you were mad at me. She figured you going off to Korea you wanted to be by yourself and walk around. I tell her, Doina, he's just going out on the boardwalk he says he's looking for a going-away present. Doina, she says, it's you should be buying Franklin the going-away gift, she says this,

he's the one going away. He's the one going off to fight. Mom wasn't too crazy about you joining up either. She telling me to go to dances at the armory. Mi rumpi i gambi i primu chi vaio la.
FRANKLIN. How many times I have to tell you, I don't want you talking in Italian.
EFFIE. Sorry Franklin.
FRANKLIN. You know I hate that.
EFFIE. Yeah.
FRANKLIN. Your mother, cursing at me in Italian, she knows I don't know what she's talking about.
EFFIE. She loves you Franklin.
FRANKLIN. Effie.
EFFIE. Well, sometimes she's afraid of you.
FRANKLIN. Gimme a break. What's she want from me? I married you. I work hard. I feed you. I buy you presents.
EFFIE. I know.
FRANKLIN. I bring you flowers. It's not your birthday or anything, but I bring you home things. We go to Atlantic City. I even took you on the Staten Island Ferry, but does she understand this? Never again. I don't want to go back there.
EFFIE. Now stop.
FRANKLIN. Your brother the fireman. He makes me barf. Wearing his firehat at the dinner table. Carrying around that axe, who is he kidding?
EFFIE. He likes the fire department.
FRANKLIN. I care? Your whole family cracks me up. Him and Marie, eating food all over the apartment, stubbing out his cigarettes into the dining room table, what zoo do these people come from?
EFFIE. They're in love.
FRANKLIN. That kid, Paulie, playing with himself at the table.
EFFIE. He never done that.
FRANKLIN. You think I don't see that, huh? Pulling himself off at the dinner table, then running off saying he's gotta do business.
EFFIE. He's just a boy, Franklin.
FRANKLIN. A sick person, that's what he is. An eight year old kid doing that. Your mother, she sees. Runs into the kitchen and makes all this coffee. Nobody wants any coffee but she runs

into the kitchen. You know why? 'Cause she's ashamed of her own son.

EFFIE. Why you so mean Franklin?

FRANKLIN. Sometimes I'm glad I don't have to go back there. Sometimes I'm glad I'm going to Korea.

EFFIE. You come home a big hero. (*Pause.*)

FRANKLIN. I'm really tired Effie, let's go home.

EFFIE. They're going to turn on all the lights soon. You promised.

FRANKLIN. I know.

EFFIE. You said we could stay till the arcade was all lit up, you told me.

FRANKLIN. I thought you didn't feel well.

EFFIE. But you know we make this big trip on the bus, we should stay till they turn on the lights. (*Pause.*) So what you get me?

FRANKLIN. When?

EFFIE. You. You told me you got me something.

FRANKLIN. It's stupid now.

EFFIE. Let me see. (*Franklin rolls up his right sleeve.*)

FRANKLIN. Here, look.

EFFIE. That's your arm, ain't it?

FRANKLIN. On my arm.

EFFIE. You got a tattoo.

FRANKLIN. Yeah, I got a tattoo.

EFFIE. Why'd you do that?

FRANKLIN. I thought you'd like it. See it's got a heart with your name on it. I figured I'd wear your name with me when I go to Korea, then see, I'd be thinking about you and the other guys would see how much we're in love. (*Pause.*)

EFFIE. That's nice, Franklin. That's a very nice present. (*They kiss.*)

FRANKLIN. I think we should go home. (*Pause.*) When I get back, Effie, boy are we gonna do things. See, then we can have a car. A big car, we don't have to ride the bus ever again. We fix up our kitchen, people they come to our place for dinner. You fix a nice dinner in your new kitchen, and then see, people they sit down at our table, they put real napkins in their laps. We finish dinner, we go to the living room, we sit on a new couch, I buy. This is a new couch, not some used job from your Uncle in the furniture business, this is a new couch I buy. Then we all watch something on television.

EFFIE. We gonna get a television?

FRANKLIN. Why not? I come home from work, we have dinner, we watch television.

EFFIE. When are we getting a television?

FRANKLIN. This is after I get back.

EFFIE. Oh. Okay.

FRANKLIN. I'm gonna do all these things for you Effie. (*Pause, kisses her. Looking around.*) Let's go home now.

EFFIE. We should find Doina.

FRANKLIN. Doina'll find her own way home. Let's go. Don't look at me like that, Effie, huh?

EFFIE. What? What I do now?

FRANKLIN. Just please don't look at me like that.

EFFIE. What you got against Doina?

FRANKLIN. Doina, her whole world is sitting in the five and ten, having a coffee, eating some shitty macaroni and cheese. She don't read a newspaper, she don't add numbers, we can do better than that, huh? We are gonna do things. Lots of things. You see, I get back, we do things. You want a Cracker Jack for the bus?

EFFIE. You shouldn't call her stupid. She's my best friend, Franklin. She's the first one in her family to finish school.

FRANKLIN. So what? What do you know about the world? You gotta know things about the world. I'm going off to fight. Look, I'll get your Cracker Jack and we'll go home. (*Walking off.*) Christ, what do you even know about Korea?

EFFIE. I know plenty about Korea. (*A large map of Korea flies in.*) At the beginning of 1953, ground activity along the Main Line of Resistance or MLR in Korea, above the 38th parallel, had almost come to a standstill. To the north of the front, between the two armies numbering about a million men, the general communist position remained unchanged. South of the line the 8th Army Corps boundaries remained unaltered. The popular songs of the day were "Autumn in New York" and "How Much is That Doggie in the Window." The biggest grossing movie was "The Robe." My favorite motion picture of all time is "It's a Wonderful Life" starring Jimmy Stewart and Donna Reed. Doina and I saw it four times when it first came out, and we cried at the ending every time. And we both thought Jimmy Stewart should have won the Academy Award for it, because he was really good, and you had to fall in love with him, even when he had been drinking and he lost all his money and he comes home on Christmas Eve with all that snow and soft lights and he yelled at his wife Donna Reed and his kids and then slammed the piano while one kid was singing Christmas carols in this beautiful high voice that little children have.

In April of 1953, the Chinese began an offensive on an area designated as Hill 234, otherwise known as Pork Chop Hill. On the night of April 16, between ten and eleven p.m., two full assault companies of Chinese infantry left Hasakol, jogged across the rocky valley area, and attacked the lower slopes of Pork Chop Hill without anyone knowing of their arrival. Also, I loved the part in "It's A Wonderful Life" where Jimmy Stewart comes back to life at the end and he grabs the bannister and it breaks off and he says, "Mary, look at you. Look at all of you. God love-ya."

Two hours before midnight on July 6, a huge Chinese barrage rained down on the 7th Division, concentrating in the vicinity of Pork Chop Hill, now held by the first battalion, 17th regiment. Among those wounded in that barrage was a private first class Franklin Clagg from Morristown, New Jersey.

I received a telegram on July 8th that he was wounded and would be sent home. On the morning of July 11th, after heavy casualties, General Taylor ordered his men to withdraw. Sixteen days later the armistice was signed. All sacrifices to hold Pork Chop Hill for the last four months were in vain. This place looks so beautiful when they turn on all the lights. (*Lights dim.*)

Scene Two

Seoul, Korea. 1953. A hospital ward room. Tod, a hospital orderly dressed in white, chain smokes. Franklin enters carrying footlocker, his right sleeve pinned to his shoulder.

TOD. Today's the day.
FRANKLIN. Yes.
TOD. Where's home dogface?

FRANKLIN. New Jersey. (*Pause.*)
TOD. Does she know?
FRANKLIN. Effie?
TOD. That her name?
FRANKLIN. Yeah, that's it.
TOD. Effie, she know about—
FRANKLIN. No.
TOD. It's not your nuts, thank the Lord.
FRANKLIN. I guess.
TOD. The nuts, that's bad. 'Course both legs, that's bad too. Both of anything, you lose out see. Both arms, both legs, that's bad. Both nuts, you have a problem. You want a comic book? For the plane ride?
FRANKLIN. No thanks.
TOD. I already read it. Twice. (*Pause.*) How old you think I am? Huh? How old? Go ahead, you guess.
FRANKLIN. Shit, I don't know.
TOD. Go ahead, you guess. You wouldn't ever guess right. (*Leans closer.*) I am seventeen years old. I fucking fooled everybody. I joined up. I wasn't nothing but sixteen and a half and I been in Korea four months now, and last week I turned all of seventeen and nobody the wiser except me and you 'cause I just told you.
FRANKLIN. Good for you.
TOD. Ain't nobody the wiser.
FRANKLIN. That you're seventeen. You proud of that, huh?
TOD. Shit yes. I'm over here to kill me some gooks, well, North Korea gooks, commies, that's why we're all here, ain't it?
FRANKLIN. (*Sighs.*) Kill commies, that's it.
TOD. 'Cause that's what I'm planning on doing before I get out of here. Kill some people god love 'em.
FRANKLIN. I think it has something to do with world domination.
TOD. That and the menace of International Socialism. When them North Koreans invaded this land 25 June, 1950, this was an announcement of their intentions of world domination by means of force.
FRANKLIN. Okay . . .
TOD. I am not ignorant of the facts embracing the situation. I read TIME, LIFE, LOOK, READERS DIGEST, BOY'S

LIFE, TRUE CONFESSIONS, FIELD AND STREAM, GUNS AND AMMO, HARPERS, SATURDAY EVENING POST, THE NEW REPUBLIC, CAPTAIN AMERICA, HOLIDAY, SUPERMAN, BATMAN, YALE LAW REVIEW, AMERICAN MEDICAL JOURNAL, MUSCLEMAN, DETECTIVE, REDBOOK, BAZAAR, JIZZ MAGAZINE, PHOTOPLAY, NATIONAL GEOGRAPHIC, BICYCLE MONTHLY, STARS AND STRIPES, IBSEN QUARTERLY, THEATRE ARTS, SCREAMING EAGLES, TOTAL SURGERY, THE MIRROR, THE SUN-TIMES, THE WASHINGTON POST, THE EXAMINER, THE DAILY PLANET, PUBLISHER'S WEEKLY, VARIETY, SHOE NEWS, LOCKSMITH, DOUCHE BAG, NORWEGIAN FICTION, ABORTION REVIEW, GIRDLE GAZETTE, STAMPS FOR CHAMPS, LANGUAGE, JUGGS, PUSSY PROSE, THE CATHOLIC LAYMAN DIGEST, LACES AND RACES, UP BOSCO BOULEVARD, PENS, CHICAGO REVIEW, AMERICAN REALISM, COCKS AND SOCKS, THE SHADOW, JUNIOR G-MAN, THE BOSTON GLOBE, CLIT, THE YELLOW PAGES . . . THE KENYON REVIEW, MARTYR OF THE MONTH, CROSSWORD, STIFF, JAIL BAIT QUARTERLY, PIG LATIN, SHAZAM, THE MIRROR, THE PARIS HERALD-TRIBUNE, INSEAM NEWS, HEMORRHOID, and NEWSWEEK. (*Pause.*) So I know whereof I speak. You want a life saver?

FRANKLIN. No thanks.

TOD. Suit yourself.

FRANKLIN. Thank you.

TOD. One thing about working in the hospital, you get to read a lot. A lot of time to read, and everybody always leaves me their stuff. Magazines, newspapers, flowers, candy, food and stuff people send 'em. I got me a shoebox full of letters and get-well cards and pictures of naked girls people leave here. Can't take everything with them when they get shipped home, leave it here for me. Finders keepers, I say. I got quite a collection. Playing cards, rubbers, packs of gum, all kinds of things. I didn't used to smoke at all, now I smoke like the devil himself, three packs a day. 'Course I sell a lot of the shit on the black market so's I make out like a bandit most of the time. Got three

gook girls working for me, don't nobody the wiser, they so beautiful, and smile and pretend they speak the American pretty good, so I give them plenty of money, cause the stuff it sells fast and they do a good job and I love 'em. When they old enough, shit I guess I send for 'em from the states, raise 'em like my own kids I love 'em so much. I don't let anybody fuck 'em see, I ain't no pimp. This is strictly business. You want any drugs, any pain killers, something like that for the trip home?
FRANKLIN. No thanks.
TOD. Suit yourself.
FRANKLIN. I think I should go now.
TOD. Fine by me. It sure was nice talking to you.
FRANKLIN. You bet.
TOD. I love the army. The army been all right by me. Make me feel like something. Back where I come from, all I feel like is Death taking a shit. Got this grandfather, you know? He look after me. I done something he don't like, he got this cane, you turn your back on him, whizzWHACK, he slaps that cane across your shins. Glad to see the last of him. (*Pause.*) He look after me, huh. Since my folks take off. Then I took off. (*Pause.*)
FRANKLIN. What are you gonna do after this?
TOD. Oh, sell things.
FRANKLIN. Whattya gonna sell?
TOD. Something big, something people want. No, something they need. Something they gotta have.
FRANKLIN. So sell me an arm.
TOD. Come on.
FRANKLIN. Sell me an arm, somebody else a leg. Get yourself a stack of arms and legs, plastic limbs, warehouses full. Sell it, make a profit. It's a good time. War time. Lots of people getting blown apart. Look at me.
TOD. Yeah.
FRANKLIN. So you can sell limbs. But lots of them.
TOD. Possible. It's a possibility. Now that I think about it, it does ring true. It has scope, you know.
FRANKLIN. Hey . . .
TOD. Hey hey hey, you could help me out. Be my front man, talk to people. You walk into their offices, they see you missing that arm, make them real nervous, they buy a lot from us. Sign on the line. Warehouses full.

FRANKLIN. Look, I was just kidding.
TOD. We're gonna be filthy rich.
FRANKLIN. Take it easy.
TOD. We're gonna show everybody, huh. We'll show 'em. Make 'em eat their words. (*Jeep horn off.*)
FRANKLIN. Hey, my ride is here. I gotta go.
TOD. Listen, say hi to Effie. Tell her I'm really sorry about the arm.
FRANKLIN. Sure. (*Franklin picks up footlocker.*)
TOD. When I get back, we'll have lunch somewhere right, I'll buy, okay? We'll get drunk and tell stories about the war and tell everybody else to go fuck themselves.
FRANKLIN. Good luck. (*Franklin exits.*)
TOD. Dumb turkey. (*Lights dim.*)

Scene Three

Fort Dix Military Airfield. Fall 1953. A section of chain wire fence and a sign indicating a military airfield. In the darkness we hear the sound of a propellor transport plane. It is very loud. The lights fade up on Franklin in uniform, his sleeve pinned to his jacket. Effie stands holding a box of candy. She wears a stylish dress.

EFFIE. Hi Franklin!
FRANKLIN. Hi Effie!
EFFIE. You look good, Franklin.
FRANKLIN. Thanks. (*Pause.*)
EFFIE. Hey, I brought you some salt water taffy.
FRANKLIN. From Atlantic City?
EFFIE. You bet.
FRANKLIN. Nice. (*Pause.*)
EFFIE. They feed you enough in the hospital?
FRANKLIN. Why do you ask?
EFFIE. You look a little thin.
FRANKLIN. I lost some weight. The arm.
EFFIE. Stop.
FRANKLIN. That's probably why I look different.
EFFIE. I'm used to it already.

FRANKLIN. Hey, it's okay. (*Pause.*) They tell you it takes time. To adjust. You lose a limb, this takes time to adjust. I talked to some people.

EFFIE. Were they nice people?

FRANKLIN. They were okay. Mostly other guys who were missing things, arms, legs, fingers. Some guys got it much worse than me, you know.

EFFIE. Uh huh.

FRANKLIN. Some guys they're missing their . . . you know what.

EFFIE. I'm sorry.

FRANKLIN. You step on a mine, blammo, it's gone.

EFFIE. I . . .

FRANKLIN. You can't ever get it back. (*Pause.*) Yeah, I talked to a lot of people.

EFFIE. You started combing your hair different.

FRANKLIN. I read in a magazine this is the new style.

EFFIE. I ain't seen that style yet.

FRANKLIN. Oh.

EFFIE. But I don't read magazines about combing hair.

FRANKLIN. Yeah, well this is how they do it now.

EFFIE. It's different.

FRANKLIN. You look the same.

EFFIE. You look older, Franklin.

FRANKLIN. I'm . . . you know my gums are acting up.

EFFIE. Your gums.

FRANKLIN. Something got . . . uh . . . messed up with, something you know happened to my gums over in Korea, and my teeth are loose and they hurt once in a while.

EFFIE. Doina and me, we seen this picture last week.

FRANKLIN. Really.

EFFIE. You're not gonna believe this, Franklin, this is something maybe you have not heard about, but this picture, it's exciting. . .

FRANKLIN. What?

EFFIE. This movie, it was in 3-D.

FRANKLIN. Huh?

EFFIE. This picture, it was like specially designed for three dimensional projection.

FRANKLIN. So?

EFFIE. So? So, well you watch this movie, see, and things they pop out at you, right out of the screen, they sorta come out at you, like real life, but it's a movie.
FRANKLIN. You and Doina seen this?
EFFIE. It was very wonderful and exciting, and we went twice in one week, over at the Plaza theatre.
FRANKLIN. Twice.
EFFIE. This picture was called "Bwana Devil" and it starred Robert Stack and there was also Barbara Britton and Nigel Bruce. You had to wear these special glasses. I brought one back for you. Here. (*She gives the glasses to Franklin. He tries them on.*)
FRANKLIN. You look kinda green, Effie.
EFFIE. Oh, Franklin, jeez, this was something special. We're in deepest Africa, see, and these lions are killing all these guys working on the railroad. 'Til Robert Stack, see, he goes after them, and hunts them down, they had lions jumping out at you and everything.
FRANKLIN. Maybe we should go now. (*Pause.*)
EFFIE. Sure—
FRANKLIN. I feel like lying down for awhile.
EFFIE. Okay. I'm sorry.
FRANKLIN. No.
EFFIE. You turn around and hundreds of people are wearing these cardboard glasses like you were on another planet, only it was the plain old Plaza theatre.
FRANKLIN. Shut up.
EFFIE. I thought you'd want to know.
FRANKLIN. Stop talking.
EFFIE. I'm sorry, what did I do now?
FRANKLIN. Stop talking so stupid all the time, you truly embarrass me.
EFFIE. Franklin. . . .
FRANKLIN. Just got off the fucking plane and you're talking about some pissant movie and why am I still wearing these stupid glasses? (*He tears them off.*) What am I supposed to do now?
EFFIE. About what?
FRANKLIN. About working, getting a job, supporting us, making a goddam living.

EFFIE. You still okay, Franklin.
FRANKLIN. I'm not okay, I'm not, shit my mouth hurts. You make me mad. . . . (*He starts to cry.*) and I yell at you and my mouth hurts. I don't want to loose my teeth too, please Effie, don't let them pull my teeth. I've had these teeth since I was a kid. I need them, and my gums messed. . . .
EFFIE. It's okay, ssssh. . . .
FRANKLIN. But.
EFFIE. Sssssssh.
FRANKLIN. I can't eat the salt water taffy, don't you understand?
EFFIE. It's fine, Franklin, it's real good to have you back.
FRANKLIN. I'm fucking falling apart here.
EFFIE. You look good Franklin. You still got all your good parts. You're not missing any of that. (*Pause.*)
FRANKLIN. No.
EFFIE. Then it's okay. A lotta guys, hey, they're missing everything, many guys, they're dead, they have nothing.
FRANKLIN. That's right.
EFFIE. We're going home now, okay?
FRANKLIN. (*Wiping his eyes.*) Yeah.
EFFIE. Some people are over at the apartment want to say hello to you. Will you do that?
FRANKLIN. I don't want to see anybody.
EFFIE. They've been waiting all day to see you, why don't you say hello, you have a beer, you feel better.
FRANKLIN. Okay. A few beers.
EFFIE. Good.
FRANKLIN. We have a few beers, and they go. Then we can be alone. (*They start to walk off.*)
EFFIE. Sure. (*Lights fade.*)

Scene Four

Jerry, a clerk seated at desk. Franklin enters, hands him his form.

JERRY. Mr. Clagg? (*Not looking up, offers hand.*) Oh. Korea, was it?

FRANKLIN. That's correct.
JERRY. Discharge. . . .
FRANKLIN. August.
JERRY. Yeah.
FRANKLIN. Out of Fort Dix.
JERRY. Uh huh. Cold there.
FRANKLIN. Fort Dix.
JERRY. No, Korea.
FRANKLIN. Oh.
JERRY. Hear it's really cold in Korea.
FRANKLIN. Yeah, it gets cold there.
JERRY. All the time LIFE magazine, see guys in the snow, snow on their faces and shit.
FRANKLIN. It rained a lot, mud, you know.
JERRY. That's what I'm talking about. Hammer is to nail, as chicken is to . . .
FRANKLIN. Birdseed.
JERRY. Have you received any psychiatric counseling?
FRANKLIN. Not that I know of.
JERRY. Any complaints recently?
FRANKLIN. I'm having trouble finding work.
JERRY. Any medical complaints? (*Pause.*)
FRANKLIN. Yeah, I'm having trouble finding work.
JERRY. Are you now or have you ever been a member of the Communist Party?
FRANKLIN. No.
JERRY. Any infections?
FRANKLIN. No.
JERRY. Suffered any headaches?
FRANKLIN. No.
JERRY. Blackouts?
FRANKLIN. No.
JERRY. Loss of memory?
FRANKLIN. When?
JERRY. What?
FRANKLIN. When.
JERRY. This is recently.
FRANKLIN. No.
JERRY. Motor difficulties. (*Pause.*) Any trouble walking? I mean are you falling down a lot?

FRANKLIN. No.
JERRY. Loss of appetite?
FRANKLIN. Uh, no.
JERRY. Any medications I should know about?
FRANKLIN. No.
JERRY. Any drinking?
FRANKLIN. Is that on the form?
JERRY. Yeah.
FRANKLIN. Uh no. I mean you know, no problem. I don't have a drinking problem, anything like that.
JERRY. Sure.
FRANKLIN. No headaches or falling down.
JERRY. Sure. Any stomach problems?
FRANKLIN. No.
JERRY. Any shortness of breath, any pains when you physically exert yourself?
FRANKLIN. No.
JERRY. Looks good. (*Starts to put files away.*)
FRANKLIN. That's it?
JERRY. Yeah, that's it.
FRANKLIN. That's all. That's. . . . okay. Right.
JERRY. You wanna hear something?
FRANKLIN. What?
JERRY. Right over there, right on the wall there is this sign, it says in big letters NO SMOKING. You think anybody pays attention to it, huh? No way. They sit here blowing smoke into my face nine hours every day. Makes me sick, just blowing smoke into my face.
FRANKLIN. Yeah, that's tough.
JERRY. Another thing, they give us really hard chairs, you try sitting on a chair like this nine hours every day, gives me goddam hemmorroids, one week it got so bad I had to come here and sit on one of those goddam rubber doughnuts, cause my hemmorroids was acting up. . . .
FRANKLIN. Why are you telling me this stuff? I don't wanna know any of this. Uh, I'm here about a job, you're supposed to find me job.
JERRY. You guys from Korea, boy you got it easy, come home from duty, you got the GI bill, you got a free education, nobody gave me a free nothing, I never got a free ride.

FRANKLIN. HEY I'M MISSING AN ARM HERE IN CASE YOU HAVEN'T NOTICED! (*Beat.*) But, it's okay, that doesn't uh affect my working and you know I need some work and uh. . . .
JERRY. Right.
FRANKLIN. I know it's pretty tough sitting here. . . .
JERRY. Uh huh. Well thanks for coming in, Mr. Clagg, we'll see if we've got anything.
FRANKLIN. Sorry about people smoking all the time, with that sign there and yeah, that's a pain, sure. I don't smoke personally.
JERRY. I'll have someone show you out now. (*He leaves.*)
FRANKLIN. (*Alone.*) Boy oh boy. (*He looks around. Sighs. Lights fade.*)

Scene Five

Apartment in Morristown, New Jersey. Old couch, coffee table, refrigerator U. *Franklin on couch. Effie seated at table, doing her nails.*

FRANKLIN. Take your coat off.
EFFIE. Okay.
FRANKLIN. You been sitting there for an hour with it on.
EFFIE. Guess I'm cold Franklin.
FRANKLIN. You make me nervous.
EFFIE. You want some coffee?
FRANKLIN. No. I've had about seven cups so far. While you and Doina were at the movies. While I was here looking at the paper.
EFFIE. Anything interesting?
FRANKLIN. Where?
EFFIE. In the paper.
FRANKLIN. Dagwood Bumstead took a hammer and kills Blondie and his kids.
EFFIE. Okay.
FRANKLIN. He was upset 'cause she was always going out to the movies. Dagwood couldn't get a job, see, Dagwood Bumstead felt like shit. So he's in the kitchen, rummaging around in

these drawers, he sees this hammer, this ball peen hammer, and this light bulb pops on over his head, like in all these cartoons, and he thinks I'll take this hammer and kill Blondie and the dog. I'm gonna smash the dog and probably the mailman if he comes by.

EFFIE. Would you like something to eat?

FRANKLIN. You notice we can't even afford a hammer?

EFFIE. You want a sandwich?

FRANKLIN. This is how low we are. No hammer.

EFFIE. Franklin. . . .

FRANKLIN. Effie, notice how you are having one completely different conversation than me? You notice this? Huh, huh? I'm talking about hammers, you're talking about food, we are talking about two different things.

EFFIE. What you wanna talk about Franklin?

FRANKLIN. Who knows.

EFFIE. I'm here, you want to say something.

FRANKLIN. What's Doina gotta say about this, huh? Franklin, he's a jerk, huh? I bet she says this non-stop. Franklin is a wash-out, he can't find work.

EFFIE. It'll be all right.

FRANKLIN. It will not be all right. You been saying it'll be all right for a year now. A year. What is happening in this year, huh? Effie, huh, what's happening here. Nothing. Eisenhower's still president. So what?

EFFIE. You don't like Eisenhower?

FRANKLIN. Where's that hammer? Where is a hammer when you need it?

EFFIE. Stop talking like this Franklin.

FRANKLIN. LIKE WHAT? LIKE WHAT AM I TALKING?

EFFIE. I'm taking my coat off.

FRANKLIN. Look, right now, I'm a drag to be around, okay? A real drag. I'm no fun. So don't keep trying to have talks with me. I don't like talks. I'm no fun. You go off, you got this other life, I know, you and Doina got this whole other life, in this life Effie, in this life, you have fun, you laugh, you do things, then, then this one happy life ends, and you come home and we get together for this un-fun life you have. I gotta have some time alone here. What am I fooling myself, huh?

EFFIE. Something'll happen.

FRANKLIN. When? This is what I'm asking, when? You keep saying these incredible fucking worthless noise sounds coming outta your mouth, about things being all right, when they're not, and I wonder what is happening in that brain in there.

EFFIE. Don't, because you're upset, hurt me.

FRANKLIN. Oh sure. Right. I gotta do something now, right. I've got to get things in order, okay, I need a plan here. (*Doorbell.*) Who is this? (*Doina enters with a picture.*)

EFFIE. Hello, Doina.

DOINA. Hello Effie. Hello. . . .

FRANKLIN. Franklin. The name is Franklin. Remember me?

DOINA. Of course I do. I brought this picture over for your apartment.

FRANKLIN. Nice picture, Doina. What is it?

DOINA. It's a picture of the sea, and a fishing boat.

FRANKLIN. Whoa. Incredible. We must hang it at once. Immediately. The apartment is dying for pictures.

DOINA. (*Confused.*) All right. Do you have a hammer?

FRANKLIN. NO. THERE IS NO HAMMER HERE, NO HAMMER. DOINA GET OUT, GET OUT OF HERE.

DOINA. Bye. (*She runs off.*)

EFFIE. You are really being difficult.

FRANKLIN. No shit. (*Lights fade.*)

Scene Six

Sam and Franklin. A bar. They are both drinking bright green drinks in tall glasses. December 1954.

SAM. Drink up.

FRANKLIN. Thanks.

SAM. Look at that. (*Points offstage.*)

FRANKLIN. Where? (*He looks.*)

SAM. Over there. That. Fucking disgusting. The definition of grotesque.

FRANKLIN. Oh, yeah.

SAM. Fucking pornographic, that is. So. How you be?

FRANKLIN. Great.

SAM. So wonderful.
FRANKLIN. I'm doing great. (*Pause.*) How about you?
SAM. You can see. This suit? This is a nice suit.
FRANKLIN. Very.
SAM. This wallet in my pocket. Full of money. Outside. A new car. Chrome. Big fins. A boat. A big boat I drive to work. I cruise the street in my boat. Little kids and ladies, they're flying outta the way from this boat I drive.
FRANKLIN. That's great.
SAM. This is a great fucking beautiful nation.
FRANKLIN. Sure.
SAM. Finish your drink.
FRANKLIN. I . . . it's tough, you know. You need a step. That first step. That push, that starts everything rolling. There is a certain amount of . . .
SAM. Bitterness, I know. What, you don't like your drink?
FRANKLIN. I can feel everything so close. Right in front of me. All of these things I want to grab it.
SAM. You can. Have Faith.
FRANKLIN. Oh, I do. I have lots of faith. I have an incredible faith. But see, what I'm saying is, this faith. It doesn't buy a car.
SAM. Uh huh.
FRANKLIN. You come back, we both do, and we got this faith. Everybody got this incredible faith and I sit here, and we're talking and I think, I have faith, I keep saying, I have faith. I'm not turning my back on faith, so when does it happen?
SAM. There's this guy. Has this limb factory. This is something new here Franklin. This factory. And there's this guy, right? I walk into this office, I ask about a job, they show me around. You know what I see? Fucking huge cafeteria, parking lot, newstand. They have got their own newstand and a candy counter. You take a break, you stick out your hand, a Baby Ruth, a Hershey Bar, a fucking Three Musketeer, Coke machines. Stacks of bottles. They show me around. That afternoon, that day, I get the phone call, Franklin. I start on the payroll.
FRANKLIN. Where is this place?
SAM. Right here. In Morristown. Fifteen minutes. The guy put it all together. He's a kid. Just a kid. Maybe twenty years

old. Came over from Korea, like you or me. This is a major operation. He needs people. The work force, it's big. Two weeks, boom, I have this suit. A month, the first payment on the car.
FRANKLIN. Wait, you say a kid.
SAM. Come back from Korea with all this capital, he invests. He finds this town, he buys this old box factory, he goes to work.
FRANKLIN. This kid is from Korea and he goes into the limb business?
SAM. Yeah. Somebody told me, the money, it was black market, it was dirty money. I don't care. Who gives a fuck, right?
FRANKLIN. Right.
SAM. The thing is he invests.
FRANKLIN. In the limb business.
SAM. Selling stacks of arms and legs. Warehouse full. Franklin, you have faith, you drive a boat down the street like me.
FRANKLIN. Can I get a television?
SAM. Franklin, this is America. You can get as many televisions as you want. You can put a television in every room. You can put one in the bathroom, you take a shit you watch Uncle Milty. (*He looks off.*) That woman is a pig. She should never wear a dress like that.
FRANKLIN. What about the guy?
SAM. Oh, the guy's okay. The girl, she's a pig. . . .
FRANKLIN. No. The guy with the factory.
SAM. He's some incredible young juvenile . . . the kid hustles, believe me. This is big time. This is great for the community, this new thing. Great. The paper gave him some award or something. The boosters have this dinner in his honor. This guy is a twenty year old kid, Cartmell is his name.
FRANKLIN. Come back from Korea.
SAM. Just like you or me. Faith. That's what it is. And the hustle. God, it could make me come. (*Lights fade.*)

Scene Seven

The Clagg's apartment. Christmas 1954. In the darkness we see blinking of tiny Christmas lights. Lights up on the room, with small Christmas tree in corner. Doina enters, arms loaded with presents.

DOINA. So a very merry Christmas.
EFFIE. Thank you, Doina.
DOINA. Where is Franklin? Is he at home?
EFFIE. He's out shopping.
DOINA. How nice the apartment looks. Franklin is a lucky fellow.
EFFIE. I guess.
DOINA. In Rumania, we never have a tree such as this one.
EFFIE. Franklin picked it out for me.
DOINA. It is quite beautiful.
EFFIE. Thank you.
DOINA. May I put the packages down? (*She dumps the packages.*)
EFFIE. Oh sure.
DOINA. You see the movie this week?
EFFIE. You mean the Montgomery Clift?
DOINA. Oh, yes.
EFFIE. Not yet. But I got it. The picture. (*She holds out envelope.*) He signed it too.
DOINA. You must be very happy.
EFFIE. Yeah, I guess. (*Pause.*) Doina, are you and Jerome happy?
DOINA. Happy. How do you mean happy?
EFFIE. Happy happy.
DOINA. Effie, I'm married to him. (*Thinks.*) We are not happy like that. But we are happy enough.
EFFIE. Oh.
DOINA. Are you and Franklin having difficulties now?
EFFIE. I guess.
DOINA. Do you want to tell me?
EFFIE. I'm so unhappy.
DOINA. That's no good.
EFFIE. We never talk to each other.
DOINA. Yes. . . .
EFFIE. Franklin doesn't like to spend time with me.
DOINA. I see. . . .
EFFIE. So, I'm dating someone else.
DOINA. Yes.

EFFIE. It's this guy who works at the plant.
DOINA. Do I know him?
EFFIE. Naw.
DOINA. Go on.
EFFIE. I make love to him.
DOINA. Good. (*Effie buries head in hands.*)
EFFIE. Oh, God!
DOINA. How often do you have intercourse?
EFFIE. I guess at first once or twice a week, we would sneak off, but now we're doing it every day.
DOINA. And is the intercourse good?
EFFIE. I guess.
DOINA. Go on . . .
EFFIE. Well, that's about it. But I'm so unhappy about the whole thing. I mean, here I am cheating on Franklin, my husband.
DOINA. Yes.
EFFIE. Doina, I'm a Catholic.
DOINA. You have told me this.
EFFIE. But it's a sin. A very serious sin. I could go to hell.
DOINA. Oh, we all go to hell. I know that.
EFFIE. Yeah, but like I was brought up you were only supposed to have sex to have babies.
DOINA. But that's silly.
EFFIE. Yeah, I know but there you are.
DOINA. So you have sex with this man every day?
EFFIE. Yeah—
DOINA. Do you love him?
EFFIE. I don't think so.
DOINA. Did you buy him a Christmas gift?
EFFIE. Naw.
DOINA. You should have gotten him something.
EFFIE. I know.
DOINA. You want my advice?
EFFIE. Yes.
DOINA. You sleep with this man, and when you get tired of him, you don't sleep with him anymore.
EFFIE. You think so?
DOINA. I have just told you this.
EFFIE. Okay.

DOINA. I am faithful to Jerome, sometimes I don't know why, but this is the way I am. You are different.
EFFIE. That's true.
DOINA. I want you to be happy at Christmas. It is the time of good cheer.
EFFIE. I'm just miserable about this.
DOINA. Don't tell Franklin about this sex otherwise your holidays might be ruined.
EFFIE. Good thought.
DOINA. So, have a good Christmas. There are my presents to you and Franklin.
EFFIE. Thank you. Here's my thing for you and Jerome. Franklin helped me pick it out.
DOINA. Franklin, he's not crazy about me.
EFFIE. He's very moody.
DOINA. Okay, have a happy holiday.
EFFIE. So we go to the movies again soon?
DOINA. You bet. (*Franklin enters.*) A very merry Christmas to you Franklin.
FRANKLIN. Thanks.
EFFIE. Look at the stuff Doina brought us.
FRANKLIN. Great.
DOINA. Cheer up Franklin, you'll get a job soon.
FRANKLIN. Uh huh.
DOINA. You should not be so depressed all the time.
FRANKLIN. I'll keep that in mind, Doina.
DOINA. Okay, I'm off.
FRANKLIN. So long.
DOINA. Off to spread more Christmas cheer.
FRANKLIN. Ho ho ho.
DOINA. See you soon.
EFFIE. Bye.
DOINA. So I am going now.
FRANKLIN. See ya around.
DOINA. Goodbye Franklin.
FRANKLIN. Bye.
DOINA. Bye Effie, cheer up.
EFFIE. Okay. (*Pause. They all stand there. Doina exits.*)
FRANKLIN. You have a nice . . . chat?
EFFIE. Sure.

FRANKLIN. What did you . . . chat about?
EFFIE. This and that.
FRANKLIN. You chat about this and that?
EFFIE. Yeah.
FRANKLIN. Very good.
EFFIE. That's all we were doing.
FRANKLIN. Okay.
EFFIE. You didn't buy anything.
FRANKLIN. Huh?
EFFIE. You said you were going out shopping, you didn't buy anything.
FRANKLIN. I walked around. I looked in windows, I. . . . (*He takes out a tiny wrapped package and hands it to Effie.*) You don't have to wait 'till Christmas, you don't even have to open it, I'll tell you what I got you. It's a key ring, Effie. That's all I could get you. It's nothing, it's so stupid 'cause I wanted to . . . Sometimes I need a drink so bad. This has nothing to do with you, you gotta understand this Effie. It's just that sometimes I need a drink so bad, and this was one of those times. Tomorrow, I'm gonna see somebody, I will. I'm gonna make something happen, I will.
EFFIE. Everybody feels sad a lot, Franklin. Even me.
FRANKLIN. Sure but that don't help me.
EFFIE. What can I do for you?
FRANKLIN. Get me a drink.
EFFIE. All right.
FRANKLIN. You look at me Effie, what do you see?
EFFIE. I don't know.
FRANKLIN. We don't even have a television. (*Lights fade.*)

Scene Eight

Tod's office. Winter 1954. Tod behind desk, facing U., *smoking. Pause. Franklin enters, stands in front of desk. Pause.*

TOD. How you all doing?
FRANKLIN. Fine, uh. . . .
TOD. What you say?
FRANKLIN. (*Clearing his throat.*) Just fine.

TOD. Well, good. Take a seat. Take that fine chair right there.
FRANKLIN. Thank you. (*Pause.*)
TOD. You came to see me about a job in the limb business, that right?
FRANKLIN. A guy working for you, he sent me over here.
TOD. Missing an arm, I see.
FRANKLIN. (*Clearing his throat.*) That's correct.
TOD. How do you feel about that?
FRANKLIN. Not so hot.
TOD. Good answer. What kind of women do you like?
FRANKLIN. I beg your pardon?
TOD. You heard me.
FRANKLIN. Women, well let me see. I'm married at present.
TOD. I didn't ask you if you were married or not. I asked what kind of women do you like. I ask this 'cause women, see they take to me. Right away there is a response. I elicit a response.
FRANKLIN. Yes.
TOD. You would not think this from looking at me, from first glance, but it's true.
FRANKLIN. Oh, I believe you.
TOD. One night, I take this particular woman out. We go out to dinner. A not inexpensive evening on the town. I foot the bill. Without my bringing it up, she hints, oh so cleverly, subtly, that she wishes me to accompany her home. See what I mean? What's this story say to you?
FRANKLIN. You bought her off. In so many words.
TOD. Right.
FRANKLIN. That's what we're talking about here.
TOD. In so many words. Another story. See this moustache I wear? (*Pulls it off.*) It's not real. I couldn't grow a moustache in two years if I tried. What's that say to you?
FRANKLIN. My name is Franklin Clagg. I'm a veteran of the Korean War. I lost my arm in the battle of Pork Chop Hill.
TOD. I see. (*Pause. Franklin stares at Tod.*)
FRANKLIN. You don't remember me, do you?
TOD. Remember you?
FRANKLIN. I met you once before. Seems a long time ago. Years and years. You worked in a hospital.
TOD. Couldn't be me.
FRANKLIN. Yes, I think it was.

TOD. Mixing me up with somebody else.
FRANKLIN. You waited with me before the plane came to take me home.
TOD. You come over here. (*Gets up.*) Sit over here. Sit behind this desk. (*Franklin sits behind Tod's desk.*) How's it feel? Okay?
FRANKLIN. Okay.
TOD. Maybe someday you want a fine office like this. Big desk, swivel chairs, phones with a lot of buttons and stuff like that. Not so bad is it?
FRANKLIN. No.
TOD. Pick up the phone. (*Pause.*) Pick it up.
FRANKLIN. All right.
TOD. Dial Cherry Hill 7-1212. You doing that?
FRANKLIN. Yes.
TOD. Is it ringing? Can you hear it ringing?
FRANKLIN. (*Scared.*) Yes.
TOD. What did you say?
FRANKLIN. Yes, it's ringing.
TOD. You can hear it ringing. Now when the man answers the phone you say "Hello old man." (*Pause.*)
FRANKLIN. (*Into the phone.*) Hello, old man. (*Looks up at Tod.*) What now?
TOD. Say, "How's the pain today?"
FRANKLIN. (*Into the phone.*) How's the pain today? (*To Tod.*) He wants to know who this is.
TOD. Never you mind. Say, "You're all alone right now, aren't you?" Go ahead say it.
FRANKLIN. I. . . . (*Into the phone.*) You're all alone, aren't you?
TOD. Now say, "You're going to die soon." (*Pause.*) Say it. I told you to say it.
FRANKLIN. (*Clears his throat.*) Um, you're going to die soon.
TOD. Now hang up. Hang up. (*Franklin hangs up the phone.*)
FRANKLIN. He kept asking who it was. I think he was upset.
TOD. Okay, put it up.
FRANKLIN. What?
TOD. Your fist. Come on, take a swing at me.
FRANKLIN. I'm sorry . . . I can't do that. . . .
TOD. You want this job. Come on. (*They spar.*)
FRANKLIN. This is kind of silly.

TOD. 'Course it is. (*Tod lands a punch on Franklin.*)
FRANKLIN. Ow. (*Tod lands another punch.*) Shit.
TOD. Come on at me. (*Tod lands another slap on Franklin's face.*)
FRANKLIN. Fuck.
TOD. Motherfucker. Bam. Bam.
FRANKLIN. Cut it out.
TOD. (*Getting up on desk.*) Come on up here.
FRANKLIN. No.
TOD. Outta breath?
FRANKLIN. Yeah.
TOD. Me too. (*They both sit down. Pause.*)
FRANKLIN. What kind of job you got in mind for me?
TOD. Okay, you ever fire a gun?
FRANKLIN. I was in the army, I was in Korea. I told this stuff before.
TOD. Did you? Yeah, maybe you did. (*Opens a drawer, pulls a .45 pistol.*) Now take a stance, fire at that lamp.
FRANKLIN. That one there?
TOD. Uh huh.
FRANKLIN. Sure.
TOD. Go ahead, pull one off. (*Franklin fires at the lamp. It shatters.*) Not bad. Now let's try a moving target. (*Presses a buzzer.*) Marty, you want to come in here?
FRANKLIN. You want me to shoot somebody, Mr. Cartmell?
TOD. That won't be necessary. Thank you, Marty, never mind. Put the gun down.
FRANKLIN. You think I can go now?
TOD. Just a second. You ever suck a man's cock? Huh, you ever do that?
FRANKLIN. Uh, no.
TOD. How'd you like to suck my cock.
FRANKLIN. (*Clears his throat.*) Not right now.
TOD. You want this job, you gotta take this slim jim in your kisser.
FRANKLIN. I don't need a job that bad.
TOD. I think you do. I think you'd degrade yourself fully to land this employment. Now you come over here.
FRANKLIN. No.
TOD. Time's running out. (*He sits.*) Whatcha gonna do? It's your move, Franklin Clagg.

FRANKLIN. Uh, no.

TOD. Now get your ass over here. You wet them lips, you get ready to swallow this big joystick.

FRANKLIN. I don't think I could. (*Franklin crosses to him.*)

TOD. Now kneel down. That's right, right over here, by me.

FRANKLIN. Shit. (*He kneels in front of Tod.*)

TOD. Come on, it'll be over in a second. It ain't gonna hurt you.

FRANKLIN. Oh God.

TOD. Okay. You were gonna do it.

FRANKLIN. I guess so.

TOD. Whattya got to say for yourself, ready at the drop of a hat to skin back a no account scumhead like myself.

FRANKLIN. I don't know.

TOD. Hey, Franklin Clagg. Look at me. (*Franklin looks up.*) You got the job. (*Blackout.*)

END OF ACT I

ACT II

Scene One

Effie and Franklin face front. January 1955.

FRANKLIN. Ready. Set.
EFFIE. Go! (*They run to table and begin arm wrestling. Pause as they both struggle.*) Enough Franklin.
FRANKLIN. Give up?
EFFIE. No, no.
FRANKLIN. Come on.
EFFIE. You're hurting yourself Franklin.
FRANKLIN. Surrender or die, Effie. (*Door buzzer sounds.*) Who is this? (*Doina enters, coat and purse.*)
DOINA. You ready to go Effie? (*Effie quickly pins Franklin.*)
EFFIE. Sure.
FRANKLIN. Aaaaah. Shit.
DOINA. I'm sorry Franklin but we will miss the movie.
FRANKLIN. Go, go it's no big deal.
EFFIE. Doina and I don't have to go to this movie, Franklin. Doina, she can go, I can stay here with you. You don't mind, do you Doina?
DOINA. (*Disappointed.*) No, I won't be disappointed.
FRANKLIN. This is my left arm here Doina. I used to be right-handed. Sure I use this left hand all the time now, but before, all my life I'm right-handed. I'm just telling you this. (*Smiling.*) It's okay, Effie, really. Look you two, you go to the movies, I don't mind. Effie when you come back, there's gonna be some surprise. Doina, this surprise is really great.
DOINA. Did you get a television?
FRANKLIN. (*Deflated.*) Maybe I did. (*The girls scream in joy.*)
EFFIE. Oh, Franklin.
FRANKLIN. This surprise has not come in yet, so just take it easy. Effie you come back from the movies, you'll see what it is. But it is great. I got something that's gonna make you so happy.
EFFIE. Just seeing you happy makes me happy.
FRANKLIN. Ya, but this thing is going to make you really happy. Effie, now I feel like something, you know?
DOINA. See, things work out for you.

FRANKLIN. Hey, things, they're the best. Really great. Effie, you know this job I feel like something, you know. Soon, we can go downtown, we can look at furniture, we can look at a car, all of these things, Effie, we have them. We got everything in front of us.
EFFIE. I'm just glad for both of us. He don't drink coffee anymore, Doina. He took me out to dinner Doina.
FRANKLIN. Yeah, I did that.
EFFIE. You don't even mind us going to the movies.
FRANKLIN. No, because today when you come back, this wonderful surprise is here. This is a thing I can do for you. I did it, I got this job.
EFFIE. The job is not so important Franklin.
FRANKLIN. Sure it is. This guy, Mr. Cartmell and me, we been through things. We were through the war. We both come back. A lot of guys never made it back. Everybody had hopes, had plans. He and I, we see these plans happen. It just took some time. Now we see these things happen. We share a lot of things.
EFFIE. Let me stay with you Franklin. I could wait right here with you for the surprise.
FRANKLIN. No, you and Doina go, you enjoy this movie. You buy lots of popcorn, Milk-Duds, licorice, red hots, gum. I want your teeth covered with lots of candy when you get back. I want you smelling like warm butter and Coca-Cola. I want your eyes red from crying at the ending. So the guy dies, so what? So he loses Jennifer Jones or Rosalind Russell, no big deal. You get back here, I'm gonna make you smile so much and be happy and just kiss you a lot. (*Sings.*) "So you both go and have fun, and I'm here thinking about you, Hon." Excuse me Doina, I'm getting carried away.
EFFIE. (*Moved.*) Let's get going or we'll miss the opening.
DOINA. You have fun with your surprise Franklin. (*They start to exit, Franklin kisses Effie, then quickly kisses Doina good-bye. The women exit. Left alone on stage a huge diagram of the human brain flies in.*)
FRANKLIN. Freud, in his dynamics of the personality defines the concept of reality anxiety as a painful emotional experience resulting from a perception of danger in the external world. A danger is any condition of the environment which threatens to

harm the person. My favorite movie is the movie "The Bridges of Toko Ri" starring William Holden, Mickey Rooney and Grace Kelly. Also I was sexually aroused during certain sequences in "The Creature From the Black Lagoon," but I have never related this information to anyone. I noticed I was rooting for the Creature to attack this girl scientist and one scene where he is swimming under her, following her slowly while she is unaware of his presence gave me an erection. I looked around the theatre at this point in the movie and noticed that quite a few of the men in the audience had strange expressions on their faces also. Experiences that overpower one with anxiety are called "traumatic" because they reduce the person to an infantile state of helplessness. The prototype of all traumatic experiences is the birth trauma. The newly-born baby is bombarded with excessive stimulation from the world for which its fetal experience has not prepared it.

A 3-D sequel to "The Creature From the Black Lagoon" was released the next year due to the success of the original film, but I stayed away from that fearing what the consequences of three dimensional projection could cause me.

Effie and Doina never made it back from the movies that afternoon. The balcony of the Fox Theatre under which they were sitting enjoying a 2:30 showing of "Cattle Queen of Montana" starring Barbara Stanwyck and Ronald Reagan collapsed, killing them instantly. The surprise I had for Effie was a new television. While she and Doina were at the movies, I moved all the furniture around the apartment to find a place to set this new television. I was informed by the police of the accident at 4:35, she had been pronounced dead on arrival. I sent the TV back the next day. I didn't even plug it in. (*Lights dim.*)

Scene Two

A workroom. Effie and Doina sit at a table making potholders.

EFFIE. God, I could die.
DOINA. Montgomery Clift.
EFFIE. A god.
DOINA. He sent you that picture.

EFFIE. Not him, his personal secretary. But it's the same thing.
DOINA. It's just like he was sending it to you himself.
EFFIE. I know.
DOINA. "From Here to Eternity." I saw that six times.
EFFIE. Eight.
DOINA. No.
EFFIE. Eight times, I seen that one. At the Fox.
DOINA. No.
EFFIE. "Red River", "The Search" . . .
DOINA and EFFIE. "A Place in the Sun."
DOINA. The youth.
EFFIE. His beauty.
DOINA. He was a real chunk.
EFFIE. Like a Greek god.
DOINA. Elizabeth Taylor destroyed him.
EFFIE. Liz, I want you. Liz, I need you. (*Pause.*) Who else would slug John Wayne, I want to know?
DOINA. Nobody but Montgomery.
EFFIE. Who else but him could push that cow Shelley Winters off the boat.
DOINA. For Liz.
EFFIE. The man commits murder for the witch.
DOINA. Does she thank him?
EFFIE. I died right there.
DOINA. Let me see it.
EFFIE. Okay. (*She takes out a glossy of Montgomery Clift.*) Here it is. I kept it with me.
DOINA. Brando couldn't touch him.
EFFIE. Monty was in another league, you could understand what he was saying. (*Erik enters.*)
ERIK. Girls? How are you girls doing?
DOINA. All right.
ERIK. Effie? How are we doing?
EFFIE. Fine, sir.
ERIK. I'm sorry?
EFFIE. Just fine, sir
ERIK. Good, good. What's this? Falling behind? Not up to our usual quota it seems.
EFFIE. No, maybe not.
ERIK. Work away girls, that's why we're down here!

DOINA. Yes sir.
ERIK. Doina, what's this we're hiding?
DOINA. Nothing sir.
ERIK. Give it here. (*Beat.*) Girls, girls, you know the rules.
EFFIE and DOINA. Yes, sir.
ERIK. I don't want to put somebody on report now.
DOINA. No sir.
ERIK. Let's see it. (*Doina hands the picture to Erik.*) Ah, yes. This is what all the fuss is about. You know, he looks familiar.
EFFIE. You ever see "Red River"?
ERIK. No, can't say as I have, Mrs. Clagg.
DOINA. Maybe "From Here to Eternity"?
ERIK. No, no. Doesn't ring the old bell. No, I think I might have run across his file.
DOINA. You got a file on him?
EFFIE. He won't end up down here.
ERIK. Well, girls, I'm sure this man is one and the same with the gentleman I'm thinking of. Works in Hollywood? In the movies?
EFFIE. It could be somebody else. A lotta people, they tried to imitate him. Act like him.
DOINA. There is only one Montgomery Clift. (*She covers her mouth with her hand.*)
EFFIE and DOINA. Oh no!
ERIK. That's it. That's who he is. Montgomery Clift.
EFFIE. No, no.
ERIK. Did you know he's a drug addict?
EFFIE. No.
ERIK. Yes. He drinks very heavily as well.
DOINA. Please sir.
ERIK. And he is a homosexual.
EFFIE. I'm gonna be sick.
ERIK. Yes, he picks up boys off the street as it were. Seems very confused.
DOINA. Liz did this to him.
EFFIE. I'm gonna throw up.
ERIK. Effie, don't you feel well?
EFFIE. No, no sir, I don't.
ERIK. Did I tell you about his orgies, did I tell you about that?
DOINA. No more, she's feeling very bad.

ERIK. He takes it up the rear, Effie.
EFFIE. Go away.
ERIK. What was that?
EFFIE. I said go away. Leave me alone.
ERIK. Now what have I said that upsets you so?
DOINA. Sir . . .
ERIK. You be quiet. Now, Effie. You are not working hard enough. "Liz I want you, Liz I need you." You are talking too much. I'm taking Doina with me. You understand?
EFFIE. Yes sir.
ERIK. Now you get back to work.
EFFIE. Yes, sir.
ERIK. Doina, you come with me.
DOINA. Yes, sir. Good-bye Effie.
EFFIE. I don't know when I see you again
DOINA. No.
EFFIE. So you take care.
ERIK. Come along Doina. (*Erik and Doina start to exit.*)
EFFIE. I just don't understand anything . . .
ERIK. You understand this. (*Erik rips the photo in two.*)
EFFIE. No, oh, no. Watching a movie and the balcony falls down. What is this? Me and Doina, dying, ending up here. Always working, no stopping, no talking, no looking, you taking away Doina, no movies, no Franklin. You telling me those things, I never did . . . I'm sorry Franklin, I'm sorry, please I'm sorry, I never meant to hurt . . . (*Effie picks up photo.*) Hail Mary full of grace, the Lord is with thee, blessed art thou. (*The photo catches fire.*) Oh no no no no. (*Effie drops photo watches it burn.*) Don't hurt me no more, please don't hurt me . . . (*Lights fade.*)

SCENE THREE

Tod's office. Chris sits behind desk, Tod sits in D. *chair. Franklin enters. January, 1955.*

TOD. Afternoon Franklin. Say hello to Chris.
FRANKLIN. Hello Chris. Sir, I'm just off.
TOD. Hold on, Franklin. Sit down. Chris, how would you like a saxophone?

CHRIS. I don't know how to play a saxophone.
TOD. I could pay for lessons. Then I could take you on a trip somewhere.
CHRIS. Could we go to the movies?
TOD. Of course, anything you want, you got it.
CHRIS. Could I have a horse?
TOD. Sure.
CHRIS. I want a black horse . . .
TOD. No problem.
FRANKLIN. Ah, sir . . .
CHRIS. I want a horse and a dog. A German Shepherd.
TOD. Fine.
CHRIS. I want a horse, a dog, and a bazooka.
TOD. All right.
CHRIS. I want a horse, a dog, a bazooka, bow and arrows, and a motorcycle.
FRANKLIN. Mr. Cartmell . . .
TOD. Quiet Franklin. Chris, how about a motorcycle and water skis?
CHRIS. I don't want water skis.
TOD. But you may want them later, when you're older. Look what I got for you. A Davy Crockett hat.
CHRIS. All right!
FRANKLIN. About taking the car, sir . . .
CHRIS. How come you don't get another arm?
FRANKLIN. "Cause there's no substitute for the real thing." (*Pause.*) It's my wife . . .
TOD. She feel all right?
FRANKLIN. Well, uh, she's dead. I mean she died the other day. I'm supposed to go to the funeral.
TOD. That's right. You did mention something about that.
FRANKLIN. Yeah, so I was letting you know, that I'm going to the funeral.
TOD. I see you're wearing a black arm band.
FRANKLIN. To show my mourning, you know . . .
TOD. (*To Chris.*) Should we let him go to the funeral? To express his mourning?
CHRIS. What kind of car you gonna take?
FRANKLIN. The Chrysler.

CHRIS. You should never grow a mustache, it would make you look sinister.
FRANKLIN. I'll keep that in mind.
TOD. Well, best buckeroo, should we let him go?
CHRIS. He looks creepy in black.
FRANKLIN. I really should get going, Mr. Cartmell.
CHRIS. When would I get my saxophone?
TOD. This very afternoon. Look at Chris here, Franklin. Just a kid, got his whole future ahead of him. Full of hope, promise, everything in front of him, that's what's so wonderful about kids, don't you think. Now, you wouldn't want to stunt his emotional growth, him not learning the apreciation of music, so Franklin, I know you would be happy to drive Chris over to the Harmony Music Store on Richards Avenue. Pick you out a shiny gold sax.
CHRIS. I want to go now.
TOD. Well, all right. You're the boss.
FRANKLIN. Sir . . .
CHRIS. (*Screaming.*) He'll drive me right now.
TOD. If I ask him, he will. See, I'm his boss.
FRANKLIN. The funeral is gonna start soon. You knew about this.
CHRIS. Make him take me right now.
FRANKLIN. I told you about this the other day.
CHRIS. Make him drive me.
FRANKLIN. No.
CHRIS. Make him. I want to go now.
FRANKLIN. No.
TOD. Franklin, would you drive Chris to the Harmony Music Store?
FRANKLIN. No, I can't just now.
CHRIS. Make him.
TOD. I'm asking you Franklin.
CHRIS. Do it.
TOD. Franklin . . .
FRANKLIN. But . . .
CHRIS. Make him do it.
TOD. Franklin, come on, drive the kid over.
FRANKLIN. But my wife . . .

CHRIS. Make him do it, make him drive me. (*Silence.*)
TOD. You heard him, Franklin.
CHRIS. A saxophone.
FRANKLIN. If I hurry, I could bring him back and then go.
TOD. Sure.
CHRIS. A new saxophone.
FRANKLIN. Please . . .
CHRIS. And then a bazooka like he promised.
FRANKLIN. Please, sir . . .
TOD. I promised him.
FRANKLIN. It's my wife. It's her funeral . . .
TOD. I know Franklin, I do. But look at the bigger picture here. Sometimes I got to ask things of you, I know it's difficult, I do. But look how far we move ahead, how we accomplish things, that's part of how things get done. It's tough right now, it is. But we need a little give and take. That's progress, that's how the world gets on. You understand, don't you.
FRANKLIN. Yes, sir.
TOD. Good. I knew you would. Drive the kid over.
FRANKLIN. Yes sir. (*Chris exits.*)
TOD. Get the kid a fucking saxophone. Then bring him back here pronto. I'll make sure he gets home. That's it. (*Pause.*) I never get ulcers, Franklin, and I think you know why.
FRANKLIN. I'll be back by five. (*Lights dim.*)

SCENE FOUR

Effie bent over a laundry basket filled with laundry.

EFFIE. Whites and permanent press. Whites and permanent press. Separate. Bleach. Detergent. Rinse. (*Doina enters.*)
DOINA. How you doing Effie?
EFFIE. Spin dry.
DOINA. You look tired, Effie.
EFFIE. We're not supposed to talk.
DOINA. Why not?
EFFIE. I'll talk later, right now I got all this wash to do.
DOINA. Effie, we have to talk. Forget this laundry biz.
EFFIE. We can't, I got to be real good. I got to do everything right.

DOINA. Effie, we discussed this in dry cleaning.

EFFIE. We get back together. Just be patient. See, this is news. They're gonna take me off probation soon. I keep my mind on my work. I got to think about work. I think about other stuff, I get in trouble. I keep thinking about Franklin, see. I see this picture of him, Doina. He's sitting all alone. He's looking at this spot in the corner of his room where a television would be if he had one. Or maybe he's got one now, but it's no good. He keeps switching the channels. He's hurting, Doina. And I need him. See, I gotta talk to him, get things straight. How can I go on, knowing things aren't figured out. That's why I gotta see him, talk to him, that's why I'm here working hard. What's he want a dumb TV anyway?

DOINA. You're not there, he wants a T.V.

EFFIE. The point is, Franklin don't want the television. He wants us there watching it. Us, Doina. Him and me. I can feel that so strong. Also, he wants a new couch. We had this one old couch. It's falling apart.

DOINA. I know how much you miss him.

EFFIE. And he misses me. Now, I know, he's missing me. He wants to see me. I know he does.

DOINA. Jerome misses me.

EFFIE. But he's already got remarried.

DOINA. Perhaps I am deluding myself.

EFFIE. No, I'm sure he misses you.

DOINA. Maybe Franklin will die soon.

EFFIE. I don't want that to happen.

DOINA. Maybe a balcony will fall on top of his head. BLAMMO!

EFFIE. It's possible, but we can't count on that.

DOINA. Wake up, Effie. Life is hard and then you die.

EFFIE. And then you go to hell.

DOINA. And so Franklin will be here. And so will Jerome. (*They think.*)

EFFIE. In the mean time, I got to see Franklin. So I'm being good.

DOINA. I know you need to, Effie. You know what to do, and you do it. You do what you know is right.

EFFIE. You're a brick, Doina. I gotta get back to work.

DOINA. I will think good thoughts about Franklin. I will think good thoughts about you. And I know he will feel you from here. I know he will wish to write you a letter. He will stare at the wall and see you. And he will be filled too full with love . . . Too full. Too full so his nose bleeds, or his hair falls out. And it will be because he needs you. Remember that. Now you go spin dry. (*They both exit in separate directions. Lights fade.*)

Scene Five

Grandfather sits in an old green armchair. A standing lamp. An old record player. A door buzzer sounds off. Grandfather does not move. Door buzzer sounds again. Again. Grandfather sits, listening to music. January, 1956.

FRANKLIN. (*Off.*) Mr. Cartmell? Sir? You at home? (*Door buzzer.*) Mr. Cartmell? (*Franklin enters slowly. Dressed in chauffeur's uniform, black jacket, pants, boots. He removes his cap.*) You're Thomas Cartmell? (*Grandfather turns. Looks up at Franklin.*) I'm here from Mr. Cartmell. From Tod, your grandson.
GRANDFATHER. Tod?
FRANKLIN. Yes, I came from Tod.
GRANDFATHER. From Tod.
FRANKLIN. I work for Tod, sir. I'm his driver.
GRANDFATHER. Where is he? Is he outside the door?
FRANKLIN. No, he's back in New Jersey. He sent me to bring you some things.
GRANDFATHER. Is Tod here?
FRANKLIN. No, sir.
GRANDFATHER. Tod, why are you dressed like that?
FRANKLIN. I'm not Tod, Mr. Cartmell. My name is Clagg. Franklin Clagg. I work for Tod. Tod is my boss.
GRANDFATHER. When did you lose the arm Tod?
FRANKLIN. I lost it in Korea, in the war. My name is Franklin.
GRANDFATHER. It's so dark in here. You're dressed so dark.
FRANKLIN. This is my uniform . . . I've got some things for you. All the way from New Jersey. He thought we could have a

party. (*Puts party hats on himself and Grandfather.*) Yes, it's your birthday, Mr. Cartmell.
GRANDFATHER. Can you eat with one hand?
FRANKLIN. Yes, sir.
GRANDFATHER. You work for Tod.
FRANKLIN. Got it.
GRANDFATHER. Tod still calls. Calls all the time. Calls to say I'm gonna die. He calls to tell me how old I am. You can see that. I can't get out of the chair. It's so hard to answer the phone, and when I do it's Tod. So I don't answer the phone.
FRANKLIN. I'm sorry.
GRANDFATHER. You work for Tod. If he could, he'd make me work for him. Mow his lawn. Clean the gutters. Resurface the driveway. Something like that.
FRANKLIN. I have some things for you.
GRANDFATHER. Tod, remember I used to take you to this fair, a fair when you were a little boy. There is the toss the ping pong ball in the bowl and you win a goldfish. I told you not to try too hard and win, but you tried so hard anyway. You tried so hard and you cried when you lost. And the carousel. I sat on a bench as you swing past me. At me, gramps, look at me, oh look.
FRANKLIN. It's your birthday. Happy Birthday.
GRANDFATHER. Dressed all in black. Look at me. (*Laughs.*)
FRANKLIN. Let's open your presents. (*Wheels in presents.*)
GRANDFATHER. Would you open my presents for me? Help me, I can't get out of the chair.
FRANKLIN. Here's the first one. (*Unwraps box, looks inside.*) It's, um, it's . . .
GRANDFATHER. What is it?
FRANKLIN. It's a barbell and weights.
GRANDFATHER. Oh.
FRANKLIN. Let's try another.
GRANDFATHER. What is it?
FRANKLIN. It's a box of condoms. A lot of condoms. I think there's a mistake.
GRANDFATHER. For my birthday?
FRANKLIN. And this is a box of rocks. A lot of rocks. And

this is dirt. A box of dirt. (*Unwrapping boxes quickly.*) Empty bottles. This is just garbage. There's some mix-up. Somebody made a mistake. They're filled with cans and bottles and orange peels. I'm sorry. I thought . . .
GRANDFATHER. Are these for me? For my birthday?
FRANKLIN. I'm sorry I didn't know what was inside. I didn't know.
GRANDFATHER. You work for Tod, you know.
FRANKLIN. I just . . . I'm really sorry.
GRANDFATHER. Go away now. Why did you come back?
FRANKLIN. See he told me . . .
GRANDFATHER. I can't get out of the chair. I don't feel good. It hurts.
FRANKLIN. Mr. Cartmell, maybe we should forget about the cake.
GRANDFATHER. (*Hitting the floor with his cane.*) Help me up.
FRANKLIN. Sure, listen, you don't know how sorry I am.
GRANDFATHER. You work for Tod, you're not sorry. (*Hitting Franklin.*) I'm glad you lost your arm. I'm happy.
FRANKLIN. Stop.
GRANDFATHER. Crack your skull. (*Hitting Franklin.*)
FRANKLIN. Knock it off, hey. (*Pushes Grandfather over. Pause.*) Mr. Cartmell, you okay? Sir? Oh come on don't do this. Don't die on me here. Oh shit. Shit, shit, shit. Mr. Cartmell, get up, huh? Old man, get up. I swear I don't know what is going on. I don't. I just do errands, fuck I swear. Old man, you gotta believe me. I don't know. I just bring the fucking kids over, he takes them back. I just go away. I just wax the fucking car. Fucking old man. I'm really sorry this happening to you on your birthday. What kind of job is this? Oh, no. Mr. Cartmell? Sir? Please? Oh, no. (*He bends over Grandfather. Pause. Grandfather begins savagely beating Franklin with cane.*) Ow, ow, ow, wait. Okay, hold it. I'm going now. I'm leaving. Mr. Cartmell? Sir? Say something.
GRANDFATHER. You know. You work for Tod. Now you go away. (*Franklin slowly exits. Lights fade.*)

Scene Six

Fade up on apartment. Franklin sits on couch, reading paper. Effie enters.

FRANKLIN. Effie, is that you?
EFFIE. Yeah, it's me Franklin.
FRANKLIN. But honey you're dead.
EFFIE. I still am.
FRANKLIN. My God, what are you doing here?
EFFIE. I wanted to see how you were getting on.
FRANKLIN. But how did. . . ? I mean you're dead. Deceased.
EFFIE. You know I had to sign up for this trip months ago. They weren't sure whether I could get off or not. But I really nagged at them and so here I am.
FRANKLIN. This is incredible.
EFFIE. So you look good Franklin. You got a moustache.
FRANKLIN. Yeah. You look the same.
EFFIE. Jeez, I looked the same since I was fifteen. Of course, I started putting on weight, but after you're dead, you stop worrying about your figure.
FRANKLIN. Where have you been all these years?
EFFIE. Jeez, Franklin, this'll hand you a laugh. I was, well, I still am in hell.
FRANKLIN. You went to hell?
EFFIE. Go figure it, huh? Straight into the fiery pit.
FRANKLIN. But you were such a good Catholic, you always went to confession. I figured if anybody was, you were a shoe-in for heaven. Is there a heaven?
EFFIE. I don't know about that, but as far as I can see everybody goes to hell, most of all good Catholics.
FRANKLIN. I'm sorry Effie, but this is tough for me to register all this I mean I buried you and all.
EFFIE. I understand.
FRANKLIN. So how'd you get here?
EFFIE. I took a cab.
FRANKLIN. You took a cab from hell?
EFFIE. No, I caught one at Newark.
FRANKLIN. How was the ride?
EFFIE. From Newark?
ANKLIN. Yeah, I guess.
. Oh, it was okay. A lot of us there took off today. Is this
y or something I don't know about? Is it some Saint's
forgotten?
LIN. Effie, you make it sound like a charter trip to
untain. You just came back from the Dead.

EFFIE. I almost got off a month earlier, but it didn't work out. Plus I'm not in so good with my supervisors.
FRANKLIN. They have supervisors?
EFFIE. I got upset at first, and thought I'd never get off, but Doina she talked to me and I decided to try again.
FRANKLIN. You still see Doina, huh?
EFFIE. Yeah, she's the only person I could really talk to.
FRANKLIN. It doesn't make sense, you in hell.
EFFIE. Well, this is something I gotta confess, Franklin. I did transgress in the realm of the living.
FRANKLIN. Whattya mean transgress?
EFFIE. I sinned a little.
FRANKLIN. You sinned? You?
EFFIE. Some afternoon sins.
FRANKLIN. What are you getting at?
EFFIE. Like I had an affair while I was alive. I believe this has a great deal to do with me being in hell.
FRANKLIN. When did you have an affair? When was this? Did I know you at this time? When was this?
EFFIE. Around Christmas, 1954.
FRANKLIN. Wow.
EFFIE. Yeah.
FRANKLIN. This is incredible.
EFFIE. I'm sorry.
FRANKLIN. I'm very upset, I hope you know.
EFFIE. I thought you might be, that's why I figure I had to tell you in person.
FRANKLIN. How could you do this Effie? How could you commit adultery without me?
EFFIE. I was unhappy. My life was going nowhere. You were out of work. I prayed a lot. Doina talked to me.
FRANKLIN. Sure, she talked you into having an affair.
EFFIE. That's not it, no.
FRANKLIN. Doina puts these crazy ideas in your head. You start acting crazy. I never knew, I'm going crazy. You're dead, you come back and tell me you had an affair, and I should be happy to see you?
EFFIE. Look, I'm sorry you're upset, but being in hell is not a lot of fun either, you now. Boy, I found that out quick. You know what they got me doing? All the time? Doina and me,

they put us to work making potholders. We gotta make potholders for all eternity. Nice, job, huh? Jeez, you think we should be working like the retarded people making potholders and ashtrays and whisk brooms and things, that doesn't seem fair, but you forget about fair and unfair, you forget about all that quick. You just try to exist. You look pretty good with a moustache, like a movie actor.
FRANKLIN. Which one?
EFFIE. Not any particular one, just like what a movie star should.
FRANKLIN. You liked the movies so much.
EFFIE. They are the best thing. Especially 3-D. They still got 3-D?
FRANKLIN. It kinda faded.
EFFIE. That's too bad. I thought 3-D was very exciting at the time. I brung you back a pair of those glasses when you came back from Korea, remember?
FRANKLIN. Sure.
EFFIE. You could be nice to me. You could be sweet.
FRANKLIN. Sometimes.
EFFIE. You could sing with the radio.
FRANKLIN. Yeah, I did that.
EFFIE. You had a beautiful voice.
FRANKLIN. No.
EFFIE. You did. Doina thought so. Many people commented on this.
FRANKLIN. I could carry a tune.
EFFIE. Sing my favorite.
FRANKLIN. Come on.
EFFIE. Sing the one you used to sing when I used to come out of the bathroom with a towel on my head.
FRANKLIN. It's stupid.
EFFIE. Please. (*Effie goes to Franklin. He holds her. He sings a melancholy song of the period, "Are You Lonesome Tonight?"* They dance a bit as Franklin hums. They break off. Effie moves away.*) I oughta get back.
FRANKLIN. Already?
EFFIE. Yeah?

*See Special note on copyright page.

FRANKLIN. Oh.
EFFIE. I'm sorry again about . . . you know.
FRANKLIN. Yeah . . .
EFFIE. I always loved you Franklin, that other thing didn't count.
FRANKLIN. Don't say that. I was a jerk a lot of the time.
EFFIE. You were upset about your arm.
FRANKLIN. I forgot about that . . . Just now, while you were here, I forgot about my arm. It wasn't on my mind.
EFFIE. I'm glad.
FRANKLIN. I'm sorry you're going away again. This is very serious. This is the most serious I've ever been with you Effie, I don't know what to do without you.
EFFIE. Yes you do. You know what to do and you do it. You do what you know is right. Franklin Roosevelt Clagg.
FRANKLIN. Named after the 32nd president.
EFFIE. Yeah.
FRANKLIN. He was the only president I knew for a long time.
EFFIE. Is Eisenhower still president now?
FRANKLIN. Yes, he is.
EFFIE. Okay. Goodbye, Franklin.
FRANKLIN. Goodbye, Effie.
EFFIE. I miss you. I miss you and the movies. (*Effie exits. Franklin stands, watches after her. Phone rings three times. Franklin does not move. Lights fade.*)

Scene Seven

A shed. Several battered file cabinets. Tod waits, smoking. Franklin enters. March 1956.

TOD. Hello, Franklin, how ya doing? (*Pause.*)
FRANKLIN. You called, you wanted to see me?
TOD. I thought we should have a chat, Franklin.
FRANKLIN. What do you want?
TOD. Well, now I'm asking how you feel, saying hello big guy, then you ask me how I'm doing, inquire as to my health, that's what we call making conversation.
FRANKLIN. You wanted to see me, what about?

TOD. You are one moody son of bitch lately, aren't you?
FRANKLIN. If that's all . . .
TOD. That's not all Franklin, take it easy.
FRANKLIN. What?
TOD. I said stay put. (*Pause.*) Pick up that shovel.
FRANKLIN. Why?
TOD. Never you mind why, you just do it.
FRANKLIN. Why Tod?
TOD. Why? 'Cause I tell you to, that's all you need to know.
FRANKLIN. Why?
TOD. Franklin, you sound like a goddamn broken record. Well, we're gonna dig us a hole. A big hole.
FRANKLIN. Why?
TOD. I feel tension in the air. Is this what they call a confrontation?
FRANKLIN. You tell me.
TOD. Franklin, I notice a change here.
FRANKLIN. You see right, Tod.
TOD. Now you got that off your chest, you pick that shovel up and you start digging. Go on pick it up.
FRANKLIN. Why?
TOD. Open one of them file cabinets. Go ahead. Open it up. (*Pause. Franklin does not move. Tod opens a file cabinet.*) You see this? You know what's in here? Little arms and legs. But not the plastic kind. No substitute for the real thing, didn't you say that, Franklin? It's all them kids. That's them. Tied up real good. (*Tod smiles.*) Pretty neat huh?
FRANKLIN. Oh, Christ. (*He gags.*)
TOD. Now you're not going anywhere. You're working for me, remember? I tell you to dig a hole, you dig it, and that's that.
FRANKLIN. No.
TOD. I don't believe you. Isn't that funny, but I don't.
FRANKLIN. I can walk out of here. I can walk out of here.
TOD. You walk outta here, I'm walking right behind you.
FRANKLIN. But I can walk out.
TOD. But Franklin, who brought those kids over here. Who drove them kids to me? Take a guess who. That was you. You drove the car.
FRANKLIN. I'm leaving.
TOD. Bad choice.

FRANKLIN. But I made it. Not you.
TOD. You don't know what you're saying.
FRANKLIN. This time I do.
TOD. Can't just wash your hands Franklin.
FRANKLIN. What can you do? Make your move, Tod. I can say no to you. That's a start. That's how I choose to start. How does it feel? So make your move, Tod. (*Pause. Franklin exits. Tod follows, carrying the shovel. Lights fade.*)

Scene Eight

An empty stage. Doina and Effie appear, pushing shopping carts D. *filled with generic, white groceries.*

VOICE. Attention shoppers, attention shoppers, don't forget to visit our bakery department.
EFFIE. Oh, Doina, I got this pain inside me, it hurts so much.
DOINA. I know Effie.
EFFIE. I miss Franklin so much.
DOINA. I know and he misses you.
VOICE. Aisle five, aisle five, special in creamed corn . . (*Erik enters.*)
ERIK. What's the matter girls, not enough to do? Idle hands as they say. Effie, you don't look too good. Is something the matter?
EFFIE. I feel terrible.
ERIK. You're still adjusting, it does happen. Now let's look lively. Or . . . (*Holds up potholder.*)
EFFIE. Oh please. I feel really bad, sir. I can't work.
ERIK. Why, just now, I came with a surprise for you. Someone new to keep you company. Come on out now, come on . . . (*Chris and Grandfather enter, wheeling shopping carts.*) See who we have here? A new face. Someone you two can get to know, have a chatter. It's all there girls, all yours, it's a rare opportunity, a special, wondrous thing. Let's not throw it to the wind with our petty complaints. Now, we must work. We must fill those shopping carts full. We must push, and tug, and move forward, ever forward. Comprende? Good. Very good. See you anon. (*Erik exits. Pause.*)

VOICE. Aisle three, aisle three, special in mixed nuts . . . (*Effie starting to cry.*)
DOINA. Don't cry. Sssssh now, Effie. I'm here with you.
EFFIE. For ever and ever. And ever. (*Franklin enters, both arms holding groceries.*)
FRANKLIN. Hi Effie.
EFFIE. Franklin!
DOINA. Hi . . .
FRANKLIN. Franklin. Hi, Doina.
EFFIE and DOINA. FRANKLIN! (*Erik enters.*)
ERIK. What's this, everybody back to work, chop, chop.
FRANKLIN. Hey you, wanna beat it a minute? (*Shocked silence.*)
ERIK. What?
FRANKLIN. We're talking here. Right now we're talking so why don't you go bother somebody else. Go, am-scray.
ERIK. First day here you're not making a good impression.
FRANKLIN. Ya? Really?
ERIK. O.K. You've upset me now. I'm going to talk to my boss about you. You're in a lot of trouble.
FRANKLIN. What can you do? Make your move buddy.
ERIK. Right. (*He exits.*)
FRANKLIN. Oh, Effie. I was thinking about you when it happened. I was thinking about you when it happened and here I am. It happened so quick. Just like that. So quiet. But now we're together. We'll go on. But together or apart, I know you're here and you know I'm here and that's enough. That's more than enough. (*They kiss.*)
EFFIE. Franklin you look good. So how are you?
FRANKLIN. Well, I'll tell you Effie. We got time. (*They kiss. "Mona Lisa" starts under.* * *Lights slowly fade.*)

END OF ACT II

*See Special Note on copyright page.

A NOTE ON PRODUCTION

The design and acting style of the Playwrights Horizons production of LIFE AND LIMB arose from some aspects of the play that jumped out at us from the typed page. The brevity and pointedness of the scenes, each almost a blackout sketch, suggested that the drama had to be played foresquare, slightly larger than life, center stage (no unit set that would shred the focus), and at an overall comic pace that underlined the intentional discontinuities in the narrative. This meant to us simple and emblematic settings for each scene—settings which picked up on the key detail that defines each locale and could be changed quickly. We began by thinking that the whole play could be done justly with a few chairs, tables, props and lights in a black box. Once we went beyond that point, the next question was where—what particular space—was to surround the 16 quite different scenes. That was probably the key design choice, since, as I noted, the emphasis we were after was on the pace and content of what was being said, and on the *brio* with which it was done. We finally chose a kind of neutral, institutional room which could be used fully as a hospital or for hell scenes, in part for the domestic and office scenes, and made to vanish almost completely for the dark, magical, romantic places like Atlantic City, Ft. Dix or the bar. The decor, costumes, lighting (a great deal of it in the melodramatic style of contemporary movies and photography), and the music that was selected to bounce us from scene to scene—all these ingredients were presentational and frankly theatrical, getting at what the play offers boldly on the page: a tensely compact and unsentimental version of the 50s created wholecloth out of pop culture and the popular press. Because the script itself and its slangy tone and internal references are so richly allusive to the period and its everyday entertainments, we found that less production, simple production, was, by and large, more.

—Thomas Babe

PROPERTY LIST

ACT ONE

Scene One

Frozen custard
Bench
Two standing globe lights
Map of Korea

Scene Two

Two wheelchairs
Footlocker
Lifesavers
Cigarettes
Ashtray
Comic books
Duffel bag

Scene Three

Box of salt water taffy
Three-D glasses
Purse
Two sections of fence
Landing lights
Airfield sign

Scene Four

Employment form
Two Venetian blinds
Desk
Hat rack
Two chairs
Wooden swivel chair
"In/out" boxes
Pencil
Pen
Placement sign

Scene Five

Sofa
Slipcover
Wallpaper
Side table
Table lamp
Refrigerator
Coffee table
Radio
Magazines
Newspaper
Coffee cups
Round table
Nail file
Two slat backed chairs
Framed picture (Old Man and the Sea)
Lights on wall

Scene Six

Two bar stools
Bar unit
Bar dressing, bottles, etc.
Two green glasses with umbrellas
Table cloth
Bar sign

Scene Seven

Christmas tree with lights
Wrapped gifts
Envelope with 8 × 10 glossy of Montgomery Clift
Key ring, wrapped as gift

Scene Eight

Venetian blind
Large swivel chair

Buzzer
Telephone
Cigar box
.45 caliber pistol
Desk

ACT TWO

Scene One

Kidney-shaped coffee table
Wallpaper (changed from Act one)
Refrigerator (changed and redressed from Act one)
Slipcover (changed from Act one
Round table (changed and redressed from Act one)
Brain chart
Purse
Coat

Scene Two

Work table
Potholders
Assorted pot holder making equipment
8 × 10 glossy of Montgomery Clift

Scene Three

Venetian blind
Swivel chair
Desk
Telephone
Buzzer
Cigar box

Scene Four

Laundry hamper
Clothes rack with dry cleaning

Scene Five

Cane
Green armchair

Standing lamp
Victrola
Table
Red wagon
Two party hats
Record
Wrapped gifts (boxes of dirt, rocks, condoms, barbells, empty bottles)

Scene Six

Couch
Newspaper

Scene Seven

Three overhead lamps
Three file cabinets
Bags of body parts
Shovel
Chair

Scene Eight

Four shopping carts
Groceries
Potholder
Bench

NEW PLAYS

★ **AS BEES IN HONEY DROWN by Douglas Carter Beane.** Winner of the John Gassner Playwriting Award. A hot young novelist finds the subject of his new screenplay in a New York socialite who leads him into the world of *Auntie Mame* and *Breakfast at Tiffany's*, before she takes him for a ride. "A delicious soufflé of a satire ... [an] extremely entertaining fable for an age that always chooses image over substance." *–The NY Times* "... A witty assessment of one of the most active and relentless industries in a consumer society ... the creation of 'hot' young things, which the media have learned to mass produce with efficiency and zeal." *–The NY Daily News* [3M, 3W, flexible casting] ISBN: 0-8222-1651-5

★ **STUPID KIDS by John C. Russell.** In rapid, highly stylized scenes, the story follows four high-school students as they make their way from first through eighth period and beyond, struggling with the fears, frustrations, and longings peculiar to youth. "In STUPID KIDS ... playwright John C. Russell gets the opera of adolescence to a T ... The stylized teenspeak of STUPID KIDS ... suggests that Mr. Russell may have hidden a tape recorder under a desk in study hall somewhere and then scoured the tapes for good quotations ... it is the kids' insular, ceaselessly churning world, a pre-adult world of Doritos and libidos, that the playwright seeks to lay bare." *–The NY Times* "STUPID KIDS [is] a sharp-edged ... whoosh of teen angst and conformity anguish. It is also very funny." *–NY Newsday* [2M, 2W] ISBN: 0-8222-1698-1

★ **COLLECTED STORIES by Donald Margulies.** From Obie Award-winner Donald Margulies comes a provocative analysis of a student-teacher relationship that turns sour when the protégé becomes a rival. "With his fine ear for detail, Margulies creates an authentic, insular world, and he gives equal weight to the opposing viewpoints of two formidable characters." *–The LA Times* "This is probably Margulies' best play to date ..." *–The NY Post* "... always fluid and lively, the play is thick with ideas, like a stock-pot of good stew." *–The Village Voice* [2W] ISBN: 0-8222-1640-X

★ **FREEDOMLAND by Amy Freed.** An overdue showdown between a son and his father sets off fireworks that illuminate the neurosis, rage and anxiety of one family – and of America at the turn of the millennium. "FREEDOMLAND's more obvious links are to *Buried Child* and *Bosoms and Neglect*. Freed, like Guare, is an inspired wordsmith with a gift for surreal touches in situations grounded in familiar and real territory." *–Curtain Up* [3M, 4W] ISBN: 0-8222-1719-8

★ **STOP KISS by Diana Son.** A poignant and funny play about the ways, both sudden and slow, that lives can change irrevocably. "There's so much that is vital and exciting about STOP KISS ... you want to embrace this young author and cheer her onto other works ... the writing on display here is funny and credible ... you also will be charmed by its heartfelt characters and up-to-the-minute humor." *–The NY Daily News* "... irresistibly exciting ... a sweet, sad, and enchantingly sincere play." *–The NY Times* [3M, 3W] ISBN: 0-8222-1731-7

★ **THREE DAYS OF RAIN by Richard Greenberg.** The sins of fathers and mothers make for a bittersweet elegy in this poignant and revealing drama. "... a work so perfectly judged it heralds the arrival of a major playwright ... Greenberg is extraordinary." *–The NY Daily News* "Greenberg's play is filled with graceful passages that are by turns melancholy, harrowing, and often, quite funny." *–Variety* [2M, 1W] ISBN: 0-8222-1676-0

★ **THE WEIR by Conor McPherson.** In a bar in rural Ireland, the local men swap spooky stories in an attempt to impress a young woman from Dublin who recently moved into a nearby "haunted" house. However, the tables are soon turned when she spins a yarn of her own. "You shed all sense of time at this beautiful and devious new play." *–The NY Times* "Sheer theatrical magic. I have rarely been so convinced that I have just seen a modern classic. Tremendous." *–The London Daily Telegraph* [4M, 1W] ISBN: 0-8222-1706-6

NEW PLAYS

★ **CLOSER by Patrick Marber.** Winner of the 1998 Olivier Award for Best Play and the 1999 New York Drama Critics Circle Award for Best Foreign Play. Four lives intertwine over the course of four and a half years in this densely plotted, stinging look at modern love and betrayal. "CLOSER is a sad, savvy, often funny play that casts a steely, unblinking gaze at the world of relationships and lets you come to your own conclusions ... CLOSER does not merely hold your attention; it burrows into you." *–New York Magazine* "A powerful, darkly funny play about the cosmic collision between the sun of love and the comet of desire." *–Newsweek Magazine* [2M, 2W] ISBN: 0-8222-1722-8

★ **THE MOST FABULOUS STORY EVER TOLD by Paul Rudnick.** A stage manager, headset and prompt book at hand, brings the house lights to half, then dark, and cues the creation of the world. Throughout the play, she's in control of everything. In other words, she's either God, or she thinks she is. "Line by line, Mr. Rudnick may be the funniest writer for the stage in the United States today ... One-liners, epigrams, withering put-downs and flashing repartee: These are the candles that Mr. Rudnick lights instead of cursing the darkness ... a testament to the virtues of laughing ... and in laughter, there is something like the memory of Eden." *–The NY Times* "Funny it is ... consistently, rapaciously, deliriously ... easily the funniest play in town." *–Variety* [4M, 5W] ISBN: 0-8222-1720-1

★ **A DOLL'S HOUSE by Henrik Ibsen, adapted by Frank McGuinness.** Winner of the 1997 Tony Award for Best Revival. "New, raw, gut-twisting and gripping. Easily the hottest drama this season." *–USA Today* "Bold, brilliant and alive." *–The Wall Street Journal* "A thunderclap of an evening that takes your breath away." *–Time Magazine* [4M, 4W, 2 boys] ISBN: 0-8222-1636-1

★ **THE HERBAL BED by Peter Whelan.** The play is based on actual events which occurred in Stratford-upon-Avon in the summer of 1613, when William Shakespeare's elder daughter was publicly accused of having a sexual liaison with a married neighbor and family friend. "In his probing new play, THE HERBAL BED ... Peter Whelan muses about a sidelong event in the life of Shakespeare's family and creates a finely textured tapestry of love and lies in the early 17th-century Stratford." *–The NY Times* "It is a first rate drama with interesting moral issues of truth and expediency." *–The NY Post* [5M, 3W] ISBN: 0-8222-1675-2

★ **SNAKEBIT by David Marshall Grant.** A study of modern friendship when put to the test. "... a rather smart and absorbing evening of water-cooler theater, the intimate sort of Off-Broadway experience that has you picking apart the recognizable characters long after the curtain calls." *– The NY Times* "Off-Broadway keeps on presenting us with compelling reasons for going to the theater. The latest is SNAKEBIT, David Marshall Grant's smart new comic drama about being thirtysomething and losing one's way in life." *–The NY Daily News* [3M, 1W] ISBN: 0-8222-1724-4

★ **A QUESTION OF MERCY by David Rabe.** The Obie Award-winning playwright probes the sensitive and controversial issue of doctor-assisted suicide in the age of AIDS in this poignant drama. "There are many devastating ironies in Mr. Rabe's beautifully considered, piercingly clear-eyed work ..." *–The NY Times* "With unsettling candor and disturbing insight, the play arouses pity and understanding of a troubling subject ... Rabe's provocative tale is an affirmation of dignity that rings clear and true." *–Variety* [6M, 1W] ISBN: 0-8222-1643-4

★ **DIMLY PERCEIVED THREATS TO THE SYSTEM by Jon Klein.** Reality and fantasy overlap with hilarious results as this unforgettable family attempts to survive the nineties. "Here's a play whose point about fractured families goes to the heart, mind – and ears." *–The Washington Post* "... an end-of-the millennium comedy about a family on the verge of a nervous breakdown ... Trenchant and hilarious ..." *–The Baltimore Sun* [2M, 4W] ISBN: 0-8222-1677-9

NEW PLAYS

★ **HONOUR by Joanna Murray-Smith.** In a series of intense confrontations, a wife, husband, lover and daughter negotiate the forces of passion, history, responsibility and honour. "HONOUR makes for surprisingly interesting viewing. Tight, crackling dialogue (usually played out in punchy verbal duels) captures characters unable to deal with emotions … Murray-Smith effectively places her characters in situations that strip away pretense." *–Variety* "… the play's virtues are strong: a distinctive theatrical voice, passionate concerns … HONOUR might just capture a few honors of its own." *–Time Out Magazine* [1M, 3W] ISBN: 0-8222-1683-3

★ **MR. PETERS' CONNECTIONS by Arthur Miller.** Mr. Miller describes the protagonist as existing in a dream-like state when the mind is "freed to roam from real memories to conjectures, from trivialities to tragic insights, from terror of death to glorying in one's being alive." With this memory play, the Tony Award and Pulitzer Prize-winner reaffirms his stature as the world's foremost dramatist. "… a cross between Joycean stream-of-consciousness and Strindberg's dream plays, sweetened with a dose of William Saroyan's philosophical whimsy … CONNECTIONS is most intriguing …" *–The NY Times* [5M, 3W] ISBN: 0-8222-1687-6

★ **THE WAITING ROOM by Lisa Loomer.** Three women from different centuries meet in a doctor's waiting room in this dark comedy about the timeless quest for beauty – and its cost. "… THE WAITING ROOM … is a bold, risky melange of conflicting elements that is … terrifically moving … There's no resisting the fierce emotional pull of the play." *–The NY Times* "… one of the high points of this year's Off-Broadway season … THE WAITING ROOM is well worth a visit." *–Back Stage* [7M, 4W, flexible casting] ISBN: 0-8222-1594-2

★ **THE OLD SETTLER by John Henry Redwood.** A sweet-natured comedy about two church-going sisters in 1943 Harlem and the handsome young man who rents a room in their apartment. "For all of its decent sentiments, THE OLD SETTLER avoids sentimentality. It has the authenticity and lack of pretense of an Early American sampler." *–The NY Times* "We've had some fine plays Off-Broadway this season, and this is one of the best." *–The NY Post* [1M, 3W] ISBN: 0-8-222-1642-6

★ **LAST TRAIN TO NIBROC by Arlene Hutton.** In 1940 two young strangers share a seat on a train bound east only to find their paths will cross again. "All aboard. LAST TRAIN TO NIBROC is a sweetly told little chamber romance." *–Show Business* "… [a] gently charming little play, reminiscent of Thornton Wilder in its look at rustic Americans who are to be treasured for their simplicity and directness …" *–Associated Press* "The old formula of boy wins girls, boy loses girl, boy wins girl still works … [a] well-made play that perfectly captures a slice of small-town-life-gone-by." *–Back Stage* [1M, 1W] ISBN: 0-8222-1753-8

★ **OVER THE RIVER AND THROUGH THE WOODS by Joe DiPietro.** Nick sees both sets of his grandparents every Sunday for dinner. This is routine until he has to tell them that he's been offered a dream job in Seattle. The news doesn't sit so well. "A hilarious family comedy that is even funnier than his long running musical revue *I Love You, You're Perfect, Now Change.*" *–Back Stage* "Loaded with laughs every step of the way." *–Star-Ledger* [3M, 3W] ISBN: 0-8222-1712-0

★ **SIDE MAN by Warren Leight.** 1999 Tony Award winner. This is the story of a broken family and the decline of jazz as popular entertainment. "… a tender, deeply personal memory play about the turmoil in the family of a jazz musician as his career crumbles at the dawn of the age of rock-and-roll …" *–The NY Times* "[SIDE MAN] is an elegy for two things – a lost world and a lost love. When the two notes sound together in harmony, it is moving and graceful …" *–The NY Daily News* "An atmospheric memory play...with crisp dialogue and clearly drawn characters … reflects the passing of an era with persuasive insight … The joy and despair of the musicians is skillfully illustrated." *–Variety* [5M, 3W] ISBN: 0-8222-1721-X